SHOW ME
GEOGRAPHY

RIVERS

By
Emilie Dufresne

BookLife
PUBLISHING

©2019
BookLife Publishing Ltd.
King's Lynn
Norfolk PE30 4LS
All rights reserved.
Printed in Malaysia.

A catalogue record for this
book is available from the
British Library.

ISBN: 978-1-78637-802-6

Written by:
Emilie Dufresne

Edited by:
Madeline Tyler

Designed by:
Gareth Liddington

Photocredits:

Cover – ActiveLines, Yaran, 4 – PODIS, 5 – corbac40, 6 – wickerwood, Crystal Eye Studio, 7 – Abscent, 8 – ActiveLInes, 10 – Peter Hermes Furian, marrishuanna,
11 – Serban Bogdan, NEILRAS, 12 – ActiveLines, Peter Hermes Furian, 13 – dikobraziy, Pavel Kukol, 14 – NoPainNoGain, Alfazet Chronicles, 16 – Maquiladora,
lukpedclub, 17 – Maquiladora, Gaidamashchuk, 18 – StockSmartStart, 19 – Erik Svoboda, Paul Baldie, 20 – GraphicsRF, 21 – BlueRingMedia, 22 – GraphicsRF,
Lorelyn Medina, RomanByhalets.
Images are courtesy of Shutterstock.com. With thanks to Getty Images, Thinkstock Photo and iStockphoto.
All facts, statistics, web addresses and URLs in this book were verified as valid and accurate at time of writing.
No responsibility for any changes to external websites or references can be accepted by either the author or publisher.

Contents

Words that look like this can be found in the glossary on page 24.

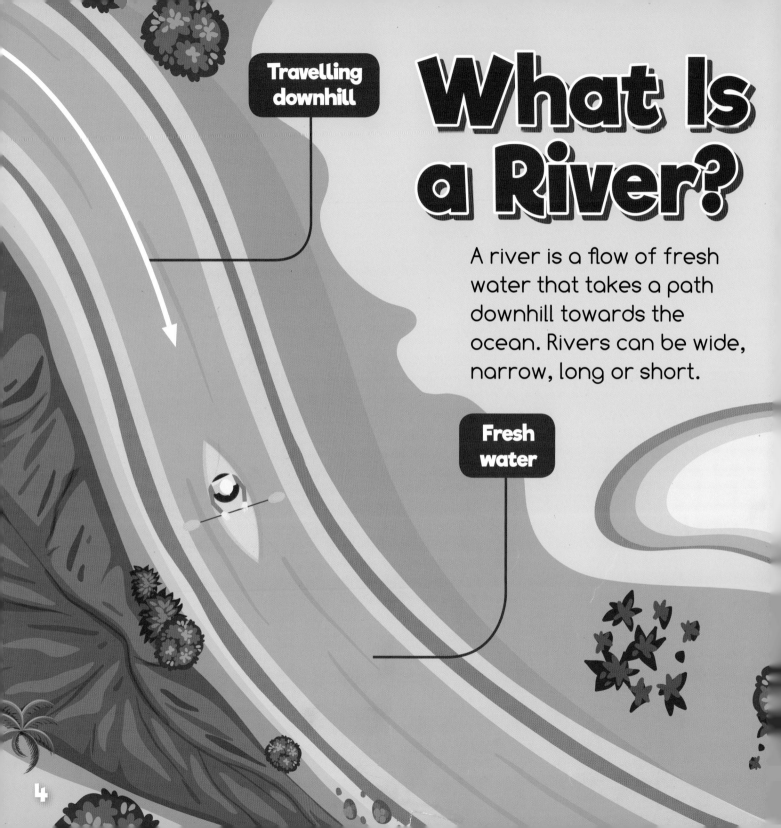

Travelling downhill

What Is a River?

A river is a flow of fresh water that takes a path downhill towards the ocean. Rivers can be wide, narrow, long or short.

Fresh water

The beginning of a river is called a source and the end of a river is called a mouth. The edges of a river are called banks and the bottom of a river is called a bed.

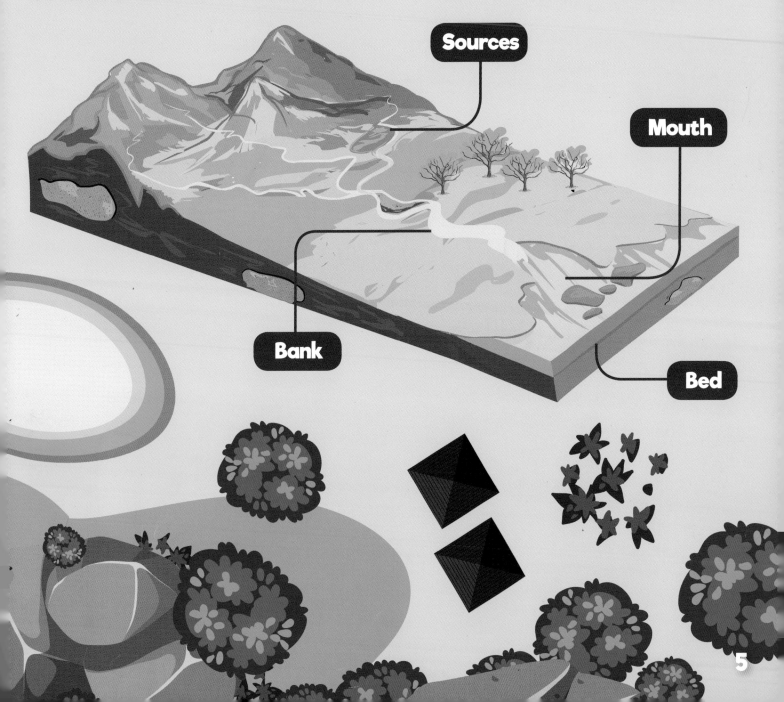

Where Do Rivers Start?

Rivers begin at a source. This is usually on high ground such as mountains or hills. Here, rainwater collects and creates tiny streams.

Rivers can also begin at <u>natural springs</u>.

Rain

Stream

Small streams of water join together and grow larger and larger until they become rivers.

Small streams and rivers that flow into larger rivers are called tributaries.

Tributary joining a river

How Do Rivers Form?

Water that collects high up in a mountain will always flow in a downwards direction because of <u>gravity</u>.

The water has to find a path that will lead it downwards.

Gravity

Flowing water can change how the <u>landscape</u> looks. This is because of <u>erosion</u>. The river slowly carves away the land to make a route for the water to flow.

The water here has eroded a channel in the rocks to flow down.

Eroded rock

Famous Rivers
The Yangtze River

The Yangtze River is the longest river in Asia. It runs through the country of China and is around 6,300 kilometres long.

Yangtze River

The Ganges River

The Ganges River runs through India and Bangladesh. It also flows through the mountains of the Himalayas. The Ganges is seen as <u>sacred</u> to many <u>religious</u> people.

Ganges River

The Congo River

The Congo River runs through the Democratic Republic of the Congo in Africa. It is the deepest river in the world. In places it is around 200 metres deep.

Congo River

The River Nile

The River Nile runs through lots of countries in Africa including Uganda, Sudan and Egypt. The ancient Egyptians used the River Nile for water, food and travel.

Pyramids like these can be seen in Egypt.

River Nile

Travelling Uphill

Locks are used to help boats travel up and down rivers and canals when the land gets higher quickly. This is how they work:

The gates near the boat open. The boat goes into the lock and the gates are closed behind it.

Water is slowly let in from the higher level. The boat and the water level rise until the water inside and outside the lock is the same level.

The other gates are opened and the boat can now travel across.

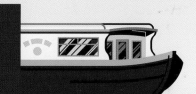

There may be lots of locks in a canal to slowly make the boat travel uphill or downhill.

River Animals
Freshwater Otters

Otters can close their ears and nostrils to keep water out when they are swimming or trying to catch fish to eat.

Salmon

Most salmon begin life in fresh water. They then travel downstream and spend most of their life in salt water. They then have to swim upstream to fresh water later in life.

Kingfishers

Kingfishers are brightly-coloured birds. They catch fish by swooping down from branches and catching them in their beaks.

Beavers

Beavers live in burrows near rivers or lakes. Sometimes they build <u>dams</u> out of wood to turn rivers and streams into large ponds.

Waterfalls

A waterfall is when a river or stream flows over a high <u>vertical</u> drop and sometimes into a pool of water.

Niagara Falls

Niagara Falls is made up of three different waterfalls: Horseshoe Falls, American Falls and Bridal Veil Falls.

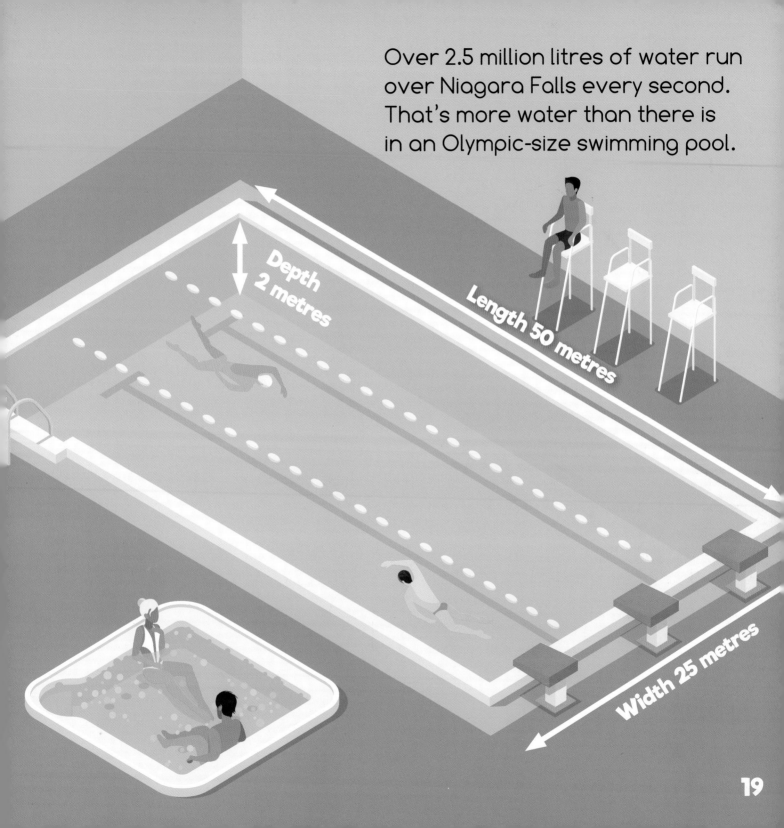

Over 2.5 million litres of water run over Niagara Falls every second. That's more water than there is in an Olympic-size swimming pool.

Depth 2 metres

Length 50 metres

Width 25 metres

Underground Rivers

Rivers don't have to be on top of the ground. Some rivers can flow underground as well. This might happen naturally, or they might be <u>human-made</u>.

Some rivers in cities such as London and New York are forced underground to make more room.

The Puerto Princesa Underground River is around eight kilometres long. The cave surrounding the underground river has many rock <u>formations</u>, such as stalactites and stalagmites.

Stalactites

Stalagmites

Puerto Princesa Underground River is in the Philippines.

What Can You Find?

Go to a river near you and try out these activities.

Can you name which part of the river is the bed and which is the bank?

Throw a stick into the river to find out how fast, and which way, it is flowing.

Take a notepad and pencil with you to draw pictures of any animals you might see.

Quick Quiz

Can you get all of the answers correct?

1. What creature builds dams from wood?

2. What countries does the River Ganges flow through?

3. What is the name for a small stream that joins a larger river?

4. How long is the Yangtze River in China?

5. Where is the Puerto Princesa Underground River?

1. Beaver, 2. India and Bangladesh, 3. Tributary, 4. 6,300 kilometres, 5. The Philippines

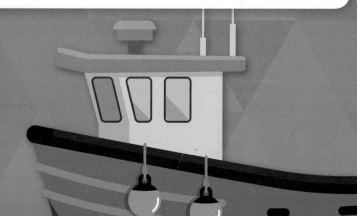

23

Glossary

dams   barriers that hold back the water in a river or stream

erosion   the wearing away of the Earth's surface by wind or water

formations   shapes or patterns

gravity   the force that pulls everything downwards towards the centre of the Earth

human-made made by humans; not natural

landscape   how the land is laid out

natural springs places in nature where fresh water comes to the surface of the Earth

religious   relating to or believing in a religion

sacred   connected to a god or gods

vertical   straight up and down

Index